Title Page

I0492555

Pro Dasher

Copyright

ISBN:
ISBN-13:

Foreword

Foreword

I started dashing in January 2020. At the time, I was simply curious about the whole 'gig economy' and wanted to try it out to see what it was like and maybe earn a few extra dollars. My first orders went without any problems, but I was underwhelmed with the money. At the end of the day, I wasn't making much more than the minimum wage.

On Friday, I was waiting for an order at a local restaurant and a fellow dasher started up a conversation. He asked if I was new - when I responded "yes" he said that he had seen a lot of new dashers lately and asked how it was going. I laughed and said that I don't see how anyone can make any money doing this. He seemed a little surprised and mentioned he was averaging around $1200/week. At the rate I was going I would have been lucky to clear $300 a week. He showed me his earnings screen and sure enough he was consistently making $12-1400/week for approximately 40 hours of work. Soon after, his order came up and he left.

I stood there waiting for my order in shock. I couldn't figure out what I was doing wrong. It seemed simple - accept the order, pick it up, drop it off - rinse and repeat. I really didn't see anything I could do except drive faster and run between my car and the pickup/drop off buildings. I finished out my lackluster night disappointed and curious.

Later that evening, I started doing some research on various door dash communities and helpful websites. I found a few (listed at the end of this book) that gave me a few clues as to what I was doing wrong. These clues, along with a lot of trial and error, allowed me to consistently begin earning $30-45/hour. Now, even my worse days are still well over $20/hour.

In the following chapters I'll show you how to do the same.

Let's get started.

The Basics

Getting Started

Let's get started. By this point you have either signed up or are in the process of being signed up.

You might think there will be some great fanfare to being accepted but if you do you will be disappointed. You'll receive an email and the dasher app will allow you to begin taking orders. A few days later, you will receive a small package with your Red Card and a hot bag to put orders in.

Pro Tip

Be careful, even though you don't have your Red Card yet, you will still receive orders that require one. Pay a little more attention and make sure to decline all

Red Card orders. You will not be able to pick these orders up without the card.

It's normal to be a little nervous about your first order but there really isn't any reason to be. It really is as simple as going to the restaurant, picking up the order and driving it to the customer.

Your First Order

Pick a time to dash for an hour or two. Personally, I would pick a weeknight rather than a weekend just because everything tends to be a little slower during weekdays. Sign into the app and indicate that you are ready to dash.

At some point you will receive your first order. The amount doesn't really matter at this point, you just want to get a feel for the process. I would, however, keep an eye on milage. Try to make your first few orders short ones.

Finally, the perfect order arrives - seven bucks, for a restaurant you know and only two miles away! Grab it! Once you have accepted the order, drive to the restaurant and mark yourself arrived when you park.

Pro Tip

Usually restaurants do not want you to park in the 'curb side delivery' parking - they usually won't notice but I try to avoid this. In the COVID world it has become more common to have dedicated delivery driver spots - use them if available.

Walk into the store and simply ask the first employee you see where you should go to pick up a DoorDash order. Often there will be signs, and after visiting each restaurant you will be familiar with where to go.

Once directed to the appropriate location, you will often find a table or shelf with ready orders. If your order is ready (just look for the name on the receipt), take the order and leave. I have yet to find a restaurant that has a check out protocol. Every now and then an employee will ask to see your phone or who you are picking up for, but it is rare.

In the app you will need to verify that you have all the items. Often the bags will be sealed, and you can't really check. I always try to verify drinks because they are often forgotten, but I don't really worry about the rest. Just use common sense. If the order is for 20 items and all they hand you is a single bag there is a good chance something is wrong.

Once back to your car, put the order in your hot bag, make sure drinks are secure and pull up the directions to the delivery address. Often, at this time, you will receive a text stating that the customer has requested a no contact delivery. These are the best, no talking and less time waiting.

Drive to the customer's house, verify the address, leave the order on the porch or hand it to the customer and mark it as delivered. That's it! Now just do this a few hundred times and you'll make some decent money.

Get a body camera and use it.

Make sure to look at the customer notes that are visible on the order acceptance screen after accepting an order, and on the delivery screen. Customers will hide the oddest request here. If you miss something it usually isn't the end of the world.

Nothing to it right? Well, the reality is more complex if you want to maximize the amount of money you make.

Red Card

This doesn't quite fit into this chapter, but it is so important I need to get it in front of you. Never mark your Red Card as lost. As soon as you do your account will be put on hold and you will not be able to work until a new card is shipped to you. You do NOT have to have a Red Card to take orders - just don't take any orders marked as Red Card orders. Most cities have a DoorDash office that you can go to and get a card replaced the same day.

Picking Orders

As we saw in the last chapter, taking and completing orders is easy. Now let's learn how to make money.

Pick Your Metrics

Here's the deal. To make money you need to pick your 'earning' point. By that I mean, how do you value your time? I target 30-40/hrs, but to hit that I have to dash during very specific times (i.e. lunch and dinner). I don't think I could hit that target of 40 hours a week. You need to figure out when you can dash, what your costs are (gas, wear and tear on your car, your time) and what your value is.

As a rule of thumb, you can usually do three orders per hour - sometimes four but rarely more than that unless the restaurants and delivery addresses are very close to each other. Take your hourly target and divide by three - that is the minimum order amount you want to accept. Be reasonable ;-). You're not going to make $100/hr. Twenty is very reasonable in most markets, 30 is doable in many markets at the right time and 40 is a good day. I'm sure others have done more but I doubt they do it day in and day out.

Let's figure you want to make $30/hour. Divide that by three and you get $10/order. There's a problem with that. Door Dash will usually only show a max of $8.50/order (it can go higher in some circumstances when longer distances are involved). They hide the rest to prevent you from cherry picking orders.

Some of you may be thinking, "hey, I don't mind getting $0.75 or $1.00 a mile - I can drive 50-60 miles in an hour." There are a couple of problems with that mindset. First off, driving time is usually not what takes the most time - often getting in/out of the car, waiting on the order and delivering take more time. Also, it costs a certain amount to run your car per mile. The IRS estimates this at $0.58/mile. Odds are that is high for your car, but even if you assume $0.35/mile is your real cost, you can see taking $0.75/mile orders isn't going to make you much.

Pro Tip

Never go below $1.00/mile and aim for $1.50-2.00/mile. Maybe go a little lower if you need to head back to a certain area and definitely go higher if the order is taking you out of your area. Remember, you have to get back to the restaurants before you can pick up the next one.

So, we are screwed right?

Nope! Keep reading.

Like I said, they cap at $8.50 - the actual pay-out after delivery may be, and often is higher. So we need to learn how to fortune tell in order to find the good orders.

But first, those of you reading closely are thinking, wait all eight orders aren't created equal, right? The two biggest factors are distance (both to the restaurant from your current location and distance to the customer) and the restaurant itself.

Let's take the second item first since it's simpler. As you gain experience you will learn which restaurants are on the ball and which ones always seem to be delayed or mess things up. Once you have this knowledge you can factor that into the price. I have a few restaurants in my area that I will not go to for almost any amount of money and a few that I love to go to and will take lower priced orders simply because I know I can walk in and walk out without waiting. It varies by area, so I can't make any recommendations.

Mileage

The first item, milage, is far more complex but we can simplify it for now. I would recommend never taking an order for less than a dollar per mile and aim for $1.50-2.00/mile. The only exceptions to this are when you need to get back to your house or area you want to work in, or an order that takes you in the right direction, and in those cases it's better to have an OK order than no order.

The more complex way to think about it is:

How much of the milage is just getting to the restaurant?
- How far from the restaurant to the delivery address?
- Is the delivery address in area, out of area or heading towards an area you want to work in?
- Is it an apartment or gated community?
- Bad part of town?
- Hard to get to?
- Freeway or congested roads?

As you can see, most of these are case dependent or subjective. You'll just need experience. Even after all this time I still take good looking orders that go to apartments that I swore I would never go to again.

Now back to fortune telling. How can we figure out which $8.50/orders are actually worth more?

Get to Know Your Restaurants

There is a general correlation between the amount of the order and the extra tip - not always but most of the time. For example, in my area I know a Red Robin order for 80 bucks will often have a $10-15 tip along with it. A McDonald's order will almost never, OK it will NEVER, have a big tip so don't expect anything more for them than what is listed.

Pay attention to the number of items. Usually the more items the larger the order amount. The items count can sometimes be deceiving - if it's an order from Taco Bell for 30 items you will often have an order for ten tacos and 20 sauce packets... Again, you'll learn.

Area of Town

Over time, you will get to know the areas of town that simply tip better. It isn't always the areas you might expect. I've found lower mid to middle income tend to tip more consistently. For some reason, delivering to million-dollar homes in my area doesn't bring out the big bucks.

Return Trip

Where will this delivery take you? It may only be five miles but if those five miles are away from all restaurants you know then you'll need to drive all the way back to pick up the next order. I love orders that take me to an area with more restaurants. Orders that go to the middle of nowhere require more money before I am interested.

When to Take Smaller Orders

Related to the above, sometimes it's worth taking a smaller order if it will fill in a return trip that would have otherwise been empty. I'll often take a smaller order if it happens to end closer to my house and it's near my stopping time.

Don't Get Desperate

Remember, you don't see new orders while you're on an active delivery. Let me say that again. Just because you've only been seeing $5.00 orders for the last few minutes and your target is $9.00 don't give in. Once you accept an order you don't see any additional ones - so you never know what you are missing.

Just for fun, go to a hot spot and sit for 30-60 minutes. Just watch orders come through and maybe write them down. You'll see that larger orders come through fairly often, but you will never see them if you're running small orders to people. So many people don't understand this. I can't tell you how many times someone will say something along the lines of "I'll take any order instead of sitting and waiting on one - time is money..." Their problem is they rarely see the larger orders and don't realize that just sitting for five minutes can double or triple the amount they earn.

This is area dependent. If all the orders in your area never top seven dollars, then it doesn't make sense to hold out for ten orders. You might need to travel to different areas or adjust your earnings.

Example

Here is an order I took that fulfills all my criteria except one. In this case it took me out of my area but I took it because it was the start of my shift and a little slow and the route back took me past a restaurant that was good for orders.

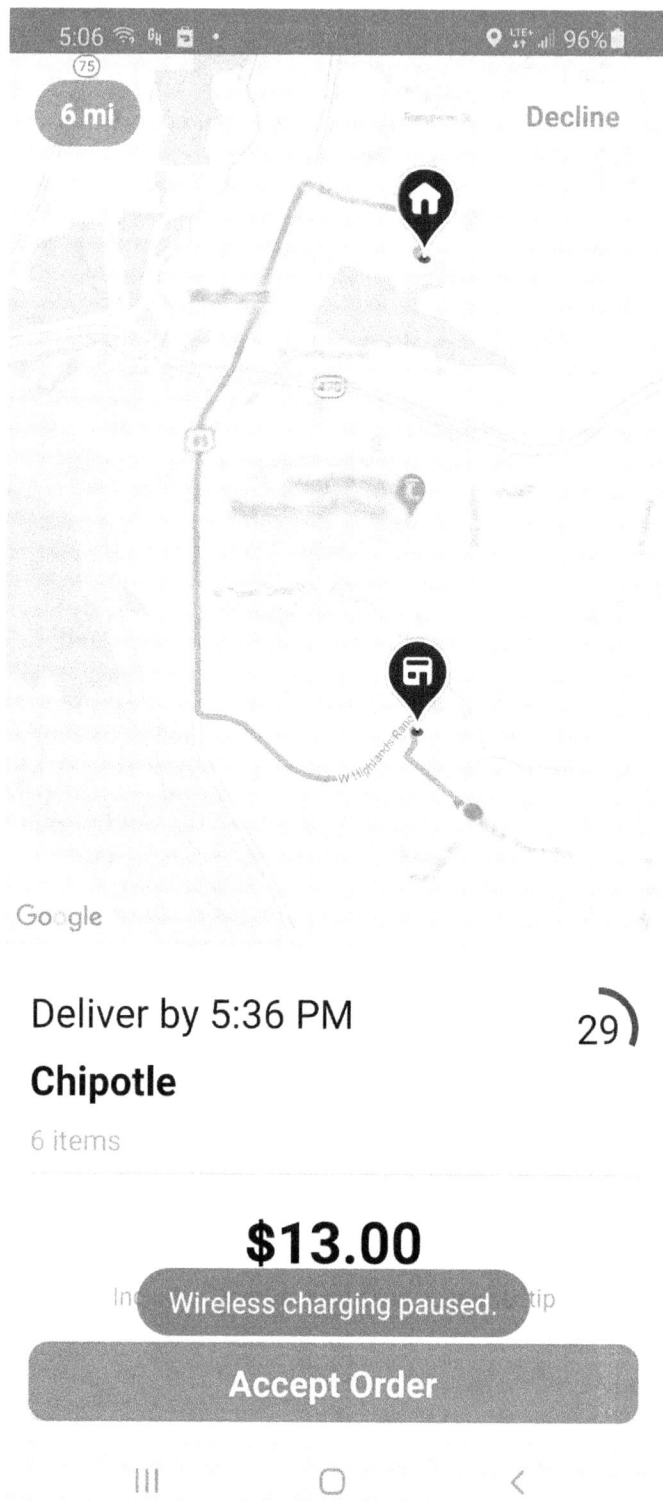

6 mi

Decline

Google

Deliver by 5:36 PM   29

Chipotle

6 items

$13.00

In   Wireless charging paused.   tip

Accept Order

Right after drop off I received another offer that I declined. It took me in the vague direction I wanted to go but it was low pay and the restaurant was one that I often have to wait at.

5.6 mi   Decline

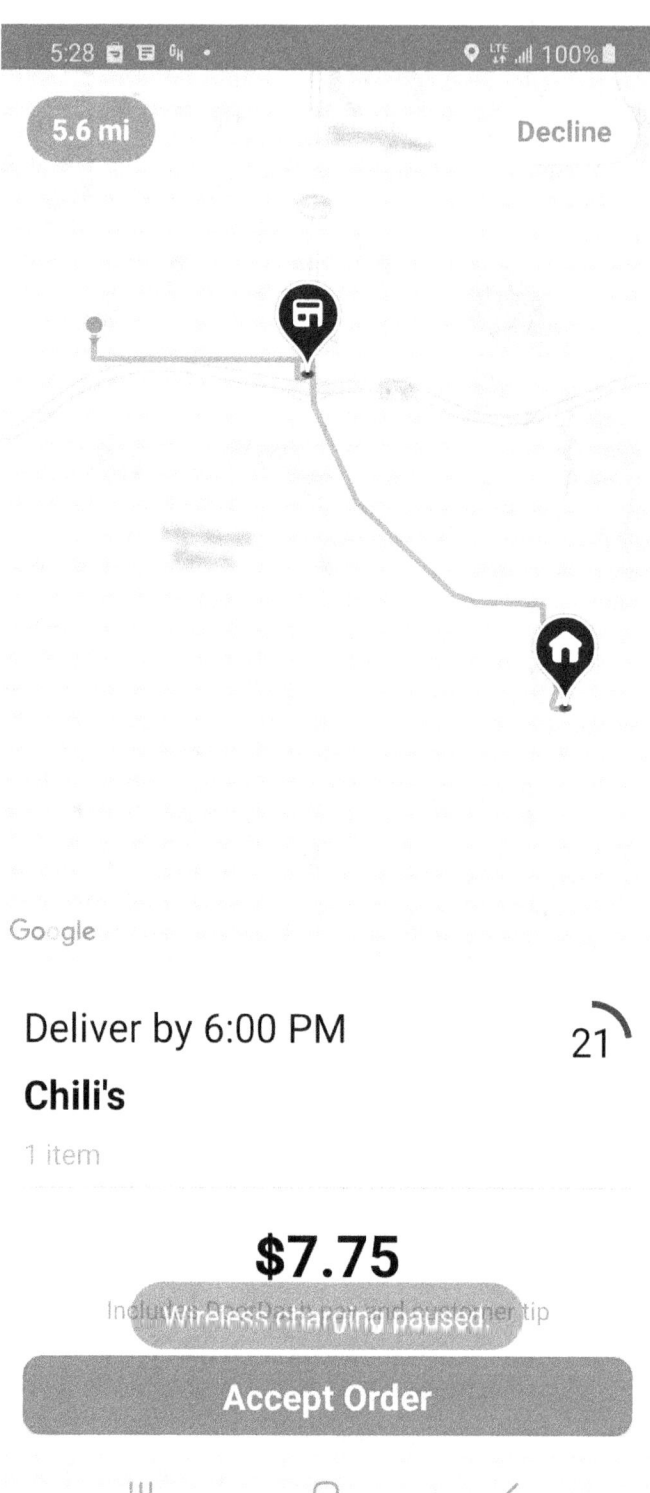

Google

Deliver by 6:00 PM   21

Chili's

1 item

$7.75

Wireless charging paused.

Accept Order

At the Restauraunt

The pickup time is almost never right. DoorDash does track if you are consistently late for pickups and will text message you reminders if they think you are not on your way. If the restaurant is not busy, your order could be done significantly before the pickup time. Obviously, if the restaurant is swamped it could be much longer. The point is that when you get an order, drive to the restaurant. Once you arrive go in and check on the order - a good portion of the time it will be ready or close to being ready. Worse case, they know you are waiting and hurry it along.

We'll cover this under "deactivations", but it is in your best interest to be polite to the restaurant staff. You won't gain anything by throwing a fit or being rude. If the order is so delayed that you feel the need to complain just unassign it and move on with your day.

Do not mark the order as picked up until you have a full and verified order in hand. I typically wait until I'm in my car. The customer is notified when you have it and they will mentally start expecting it sooner than you can probably get it there. By waiting until the last second to mark the order picked up you shave a minute or two off the customer's perceived wait time.

Most restaurants will let you use their public restrooms. I've heard dashers complain the XYZ restaurant wouldn't let them, but I've personally never run into this. Just walk in like a customer and head to the restroom - no reason to make a production of it. I hope this doesn't need to be said, but pick up the order AFTER your restroom visit ;-).

Parking

Finding a parking space can make or break your delivery time. Most of the time it is easy to find a standard parking spot but from time to time you need to get "creative".

At restaurants, I tend to shy away from the curb side delivery or to-go parking slots, but when it's busy I don't hesitate to pull into one. Sometimes, the restaurant will ask me to not do that but most of the time they don't notice or care. Ideally, you are in and out in a couple of minutes. Whatever you do, do not use an accessible parking spot no matter how quick you think you will be.

House parking is the simplest. You can almost always pull into the driveway or along the end of the driveway. In a pinch, I will just double park by a car parked on the curb and turn on my flashing lights.

Apartments are the bane of our existence. Almost always parking can be tight. I don't hesitate to park along any nearby curb even if it is marked "no parking". Also, don't be shy about using reserved parking spots. The odds of someone coming home during the two minutes you are away delivering are very low. Leave your flashers on and even if they do, they will know you will be back quickly.

Be creative and simply ask yourself if a police officer saw this would they mind and more importantly would they give you a ticket? They are very aware of the perils of delivery parking and as long as you aren't being dangerous you should be fine.

Pro Tip

Never use an accessible parking spot and always ask yourself if what you are doing is dangerous or rude.

Metrics

Average Customer Rating

Important, but don't fret it. It needs to stay over 4.20 but it will naturally fluctuate, sometimes for reasons out of your control. Customers will rate you low for bad food, cold food, or missing items even when you have no control over that. Later, we will cover some simple ways to solicit five star reviews so that those occasionally one star ratings are no big deal.

Before you ask, no you cannot see which customer rated you or what they said. Support won't tell you either. Just accept it and move on.

Acceptance Rate

This is not important at all. Mine has been as low as 1% and usually hovers around 5-6%. You are an independent contractor and can accept or decline any orders you want. Most of the rest of this book is how to pick the right orders to maximize your earnings. Decline, decline and decline some more!

Completion Rate

This is important. Once you accept an order, DD really wants you to finish it. If you haven't picked up the food, you can unassign the order. When you do this, the percentage may drop very slightly. Technically, you have to keep it over 80% or you can be deactivated. Personally, I try to keep it always well into the 90s. This is your safety valve. For when you accidentally take an order that wasn't what you thought, or is going somewhere you definitely don't want to go, you can simply unassign. Just don't do it too often

If a customer contacts you and is being threatening, unassign and contact support to have them reverse the unassigned hit.

On Time

This is important. In extreme cases you can be deactivated. No one is quite sure when or how late, but it seems to be in extreme cases. Keep an eye on this and keep it over 90, but don't lose sleep over it.

Total Lifetime

This is not important at all. Just fun to see the number of orders you've completed

Customer Ratings

Negative reviews happen; you will get dinged for things that are not your fault. Nothing you can do about it so don't worry about it.

Some people spend a lot of time communicating with the customer, but I haven't noticed any difference when I did. I communicate when needed but nothing beyond that. I focus on getting them their order and not providing a play by play of the process via text message.

Don't worry about it too much. You need to keep the rate above 4.20, but other than that, it's not known that higher rated drivers get better orders. Later on, I'll detail a trick to use to gather tons of five star ratings.

Really, if you get the order to them timely, and are polite and decently clean, the ratings will take care of themselves.

Smile, thank them, don't complain - minimize contact.

Pro Tip

You'll be happier if you don't obsess over your rating. Check it from time to time but don't check after every delivery.

You might, occasionally, receive a message from the customer for something they didn't order through the app with the implication that you will get a five star rating if you follow through. I simply unassign these orders, or, if they are contactless, I just ignore the message if the delivery pays well. I would never recommend stopping by the convenience store for ice or cigarettes - yes customers do request this!

Stacked and Add On Orders

Add Ons

Sometimes, when you are on an active order, DD will ask you to pick up an additional order. This is called an add on order. The general rule of thumb is that these are not worth the effort. Usually, the additional amount to be paid does not meet your requirements for accepting a delivery. Keep an eye out though as every now and then it can make sense.

I usually take a stacked order if it is for the same restaurant I'm already going to and the delivery is in the same area as the first order. For example, if I'm standing in Noodles waiting on a $10.00 for four miles delivery and I get an add on for $5.00, that adds an extra mile to the delivery, I will often take it. I normally wouldn't take a $5.00 order but the way I look at it is now I have 15 bucks for five miles with two stops. Not everyone agrees but this has worked well for me.

Pro Tip

Pay attention! DD will sometimes send you stacked orders that are nowhere near each other. Decline these orders as fast as possible.

Stacked Orders

A close relative to the add on is a stacked order. A stacked order is an offer to you that has multiple drop offs from the same restaurant. Usually, DD does this to combine a higher paying order with a low paying order. The general rule of thumb with these orders is you are simply delivering an order you would never have taken by itself. Occasionally, I will see one that has destinations within a few minutes of each other - in this case I just look at the total and make a go no go decision.

With both stacked and ad on orders you need to know both your area and your restaurants. Nothing is worse than having an add on order and the second restaurant is slow.

Pro Tip

Don't mark the first order as picked up until you have left the first restaurant, or if it's close by, arrived at the second pick up location. This helps manage customer expectations.

Protecting Yourself

The reality is that some customers will try to scam DD out of food. Who cares? You do! DD will contact you with the assumption that you either delivered to the incorrect location or you stole the food. In some areas this scam is very common and in others it's almost unheard of.

To protect yourself you need to take a few common-sense precautions.

The first and simplest is to always swipe when you have arrived, deliver the food, take a picture, and then swipe "delivered". Some drivers will swipe "arrived" and "delivered" immediately so that they can begin getting orders, but DD will have timestamps. If you swipe "arrived", then take a time stamped photo and then swipe "delivered" you will go a long way towards keeping yourself protected.

Keep in mind that DD tracks your GPS and knows if you arrived at both the restaurant and the customer's house.

I always take a photo unless the customer is waiting for me. Lately, almost all orders are contactless so I just leave the food on their porch. It is very easy to take a picture. Then I message the customer a thank you and then attach a picture of the food so they know where it's at on their porch.

Some dashers use apps that time stamp and put GPS coordinates on the phone. I think this is a great idea, but for me it doesn't work very well. I send a picture, along with a thank you, to each customer through the DoorDash app. I've found that sending a picture with GPS coordinates etc. upsets the customer so I just use my built-in phone camera app. You could do both, but I feel protected with what I do.

Remember DD can see all text messages between you and the customer, so this really helps auto document your delivery. Even when I hand an order directly to a customer, I will text a quick thank you to them. Since DD sees this, it seems very suspicious if you text a thank you and then an hour later the customer claims they never received it.

Pro Tip

Often, after texting a picture of the order drop off, a customer will text back a quick thank you. In this case, I always respond with a "You're welcome" and a quick "If you don't mind could you open the app and give me a five star review."

A very easy way to provide full protection is to simply buy a small body cam and record your entire delivery. When you pull up to the house make sure to try and catch the house number in the video, the placement of the food, and then the walk back to the car along with driving off. Personally, I just leave the video on the entire time I'm online. I download it to my computer each night and then delete it after a day or so.

Luckily, dashers are not prime targets. Everyone is aware that we don't carry large amounts of money. That, however, doesn't mean you can ignore your own safety.

I would suggest you carry a can of mace or possibly a collapsible baton. Check out this article for more details on personal protection products.

Pro Tip

Always be aware of your surroundings.

Pro Tip

Always listen to your gut.

This is a hot topic in the online discussion boards. Many suggest that you hide the fact that you are delivering anything if involved in an accident and don't worry about extra insurance.

Personally, I think that is terrible advice. Even a minor wreck costs a significant amount of money and almost no standard auto policy will cover you if they find out you were working when the accident happens. All it takes is the police mentioning your DoorDash bag or the fact you had a lot of food in the car.

Why risk it? Call your insurance provider and ask them what a rider policy would cost. I've seen people say it's as low as $10/month. Mine runs at $35/month and I think it is well worth it for the peace of mind.

Customer Relations

Customer Relations

Some drivers will proactively message customers about the status of their order - almost a play by play of the delivery process. I don't think this is necessary and as a customer I would find it annoying. If you have a question, or the order is very delayed, then by all means message before delivery.

To protect yourself, I do suggest messaging after the delivery. Below are some of the scripts I use. Most text message apps allow you to create shortcuts so you can type in something short like "ddlop" (DoorDash left on porch) and have it text in multiple sentences.

These are the ones I use:

When the restaurant is running late:

"Hello! This is _____ your DoorDash driver! The restaurant is very busy tonight and is running a bit behind on their orders. I'll let you know as soon as I have your food and I'm on the way!"

After Delivery:

"Thanks for using DoorDash, hope you enjoy your food! If you were satisfied with my delivery, I would be very grateful for a five star rating! Hope to see you again! :)"

<u>or</u>

"Hello - As you requested, I have left your order on your porch. Thank you and enjoy your food!"

After sending that, I also send a picture of the order on their porch.

If the customer responds to this message, I fire off:

"I would be very grateful for a five star rating! Hope to see you again."

This has worked very well for me. When a customer responds back, they are primed to help you out.

When I hand food to the customer, I send the following:

"Hello - I just hand-delivered your DoorDash order to your door. Thank you and enjoy your food!"

I do this because it looks fishy if a customer claims you didn't deliver their order but they never responded to the above message.

I also use the following for customer complaints about missing items:

The DoorDasher you are attempting to contact is no longer available as the order has been delivered. If needed, please contact DoorDash support at XXXX

Pro Tip

Do not solicit tips directly from the customer. They have already put a tip on the order and begging for more is not going to look good nor will it be successful.

I've never tried this, but the idea sounds promising. Many drivers will place a sticker on the orders that solicit a rating. Just Google "DoorDash delivery driver stickers" and you will find many options. If your ratings are struggling, I would suggest trying this.

Pro Tip

Do not place a sticker on any items inside the bag. Always place the sticker on the outside of the bag. You don't want the customer wondering why you were rummaging through their bag.

Equipment

Since recommended equipment always changes, I've put together a web page that lists the best deals on the items I recommend.

Check it out here - http://www.prodasher.com

- New Bags
- Drink Carriers
- Body Cam
- Phone
- Straws
- Napkins
- Stickers
- Disposable Drink Carriers

Taxes

As a driver for DD, or any other delivery service, you are an independent contractor. This means, among other things, that no taxes are taken out of your pay checks. At first, this will seem awesome but remember the IRS will get their money!

Because you are an independent contractor you can deduct various expenses from your earnings. I'm not an accountant or lawyer so do your own research.

Standard Auto Mileage Deduction

The easiest and most profitable deduction is a standard per mile deduction for car use. This deduction is 58 cents per mile, so it can really add up. I use software to track my mileage and suggest you do the same. Check out XXXXX, but there are dozens of applications that will do this for you. You have to do this! Seriously. Look at it this way, for every hundred miles driven doing deliveries you can earn 60 dollars tax free!

The mileage deduction covers all car expenses so you can't also deduct fuel costs, repairs, tires etc.

You can track all the mileage you have from the time you log in until you log out - not just to the restaurant and the customer.

You must track your mileage!

Don't think it's worth your time? Check this out.

Let's say you drive 100 miles while making $150.

Estimated taxes:

With Mileage Deduction
150 - 58 (mileage deduction) = $92 taxable
150 - 30.36 (92 est. 33% taxes) = $119.64

Without:
150 - est. 33% taxes 50 = $100

That is almost a 20% raise just for tracking your mileage!

Pro Tip

If possible, dash when you need to run errands. You can then deduct the miles and you might pick up a good order or two. Just to be safe, I only track mileage when I do this if I end up delivering at least one order.

Itemized Deduction

If you want, you can keep detailed records for everything related to your car and the percentage of use related to your Door Dashing. Honestly, if your itemized costs drastically exceeded the standard deduction you may have too many expenses related to your current vehicle to make dashing profitable.

Extra Equipment

If you need other non-car equipment such as a cell phone, cell plan, bags etc. you can deduct all or part of those costs. Do some Google searches to see what you can and can't do.

When it comes to deducting your cell phone plan, you have to deduct a percentage based on how much you use it for DoorDashing versus personal use. Do not try to deduct 100%. You can have two phones and if you use one exclusively for DoorDash you can deduct 100% of the cost of that phone and related phone line.

Tax prep/software fees

Here's the deal - you have to keep records. Keep your receipts and mileage records; it's basically free money.

Meals

You can deduct 50% of the cost of meals you buy for yourself while you are dashing. Again, keep you receipts - you can only deduct what you can prove.

Quarterly Taxes

When you are self-employed you are required to pay estimated taxes to the IRS every quarter. Your first year of self-employment you don't have to do this but in year two onwards you will. If you do not, you will be assessed a penalty. Check out the IRS website for the required forms.

Scams

Depending on your area, you may run into customers who attempt scams often or it may be a very rare event. Either way, it's smart to keep an eye open for the following common scams:

Claims you did not deliver

When answering DoorDash calls make sure to answer the phone and answer all their questions. Do not ignore the call - this will not go away on its own.

This is very common. It will happen even if you personally hand the meal to the customer. I have personally handed an order to a customer, been thanked, and then am no more than a few minutes from their house when DoorDash calls and says they claim the order wasn't delivered. I just send the video from my body cam and that is that.

Claims Missing Items

Similar to the above but rather than claiming the whole order is missing, they will just claim an item or two is missing. This one is hard to prove even when you take pictures. Luckily, it doesn't happen often and DoorDash is aware of it. This is why I wish all restaurants would seal their bags.

Pro Tip

If the restaurant doesn't seal the bag, I recommend tying the bag shut if possible. If the customer contacts you and asks where the items are simply politely tell them they need to contact Door Dash support and that it isn't possible for you to track it down.

Change of Address

This one really sucks. What happens is the customer places an order from an address only a couple of miles from the restaurant. Once you pick the order up they will call or message and give some excuse for needing to change the delivery address - usually something along the lines of "I accidentally used an address for a friend's house. Last time I ordered from there but now I'm at my house and forgot to change it. If you will just go to my home address, I'll tip you in cash for the trouble."

The problem with this is that DoorDash will still have the old address and you won't be able to mark the order complete. After you drop the order off and leave, they will report the order as never delivered. DoorDash will have no record of you going to the stated address and you will basically be out of luck.

I would suggest always taking the order back to the restaurant and contacting support with screen shots of the message exchange.

Inform the customer that you can only deliver to the stated address and that they need to contact DoorDash to adjust the order.

Yes, occasionally customers really do use the wrong address but the problem still remains.

A variant of this is, without wanting to claim the order was not delivered, they will simply give you an address 10-20 miles away - one that you would never have accepted, and they know it.

Customer Becomes a Dasher

A customer will set themselves up as a driver (so that they can get the red DoorDash bag) and then through the customer app order from a nearby restaurant. They will then go to the restaurant and pretend to be the driver assigned to the order and pick their own order up. Once they are home, they will wait a while and then contact DoorDash and claim the order was never delivered. The way this impacts you is if you accept this order, you will arrive at the restaurant to pick it up and they will tell you another driver took it. Very rarely will they remake the order. This can waste a lot of your time while you contact DoorDash to have the "unassigned" taken off your order.

In the most extreme cases, the restaurant remakes the order and you deliver it. The customer could still claim non-delivery and now you have the restaurant complain they had two orders go missing.

I always unassign an order that I've been told has already been picked up - it isn't worth the hassle. I also contact Door Dash chat and tell them I'm at the restaurant and the order has already been picked up.

Phishing Attack

In this case, hackers will place an order - usually sizable with a large tip. Once you accept the order, they will call you through the DoorDash app and claim to be with DoorDash support. Eventually, they will get around to telling you they need your account info (id and password) so that they can fix some issue. If you give it to them, they will log in to your account and change the bank pay-out information and, if it's enabled, do a quick pay. Never, ever, for any reason, give out your user id or password. DoorDash support does not need these for any reason whatsoever.

Preventing Deactivation

Let's talk about the ways you can get deactivated on DoorDash. This list isn't exhaustive, but it covers the most common causes.

The simple reality is if you pick up on time, be polite and deliver on time you will have very few, if any, issues. The biggest one you would face is customers making fraudulent claims that you didn't deliver but we've covered how to prevent that in a previous chapter (hint, take pictures and wear a body cam).

Low Customer Rating Below 4.2

Only after you have made 100 deliveries.

You may not get a warning from DoorDash. Really going this low is hard to do and if you are this low after a few hundred orders I would take a long look in the mirror. If you do what you are supposed to, politely and timely, the rating will take care of itself.

Completion Rate

You may not get a warning from DoorDash. DoorDash expects you to deliver all orders you accept. You can go as low as an 80% completion rate, but I wouldn't recommend going below 90%.

Arguing With Staff

Restaurant staff can and will give DoorDash feedback. Just be nice. Seriously, if you feel the need to throw a fit just unassign the order. It will save you lots of grief.

Inappropriate Comments to Customers

Customers can give you feedback, and they can directly contact DoorDash. If you are receiving messages/calls from customers before you deliver that sound threatening simply take the food back to the restaurant and contact support. Do not argue with a customer. Always be polite and direct them to DoorDash support.

Use Someone Else's Account

Also, you can't sign up for two separate accounts for yourself. No, you can't have your boyfriend/girlfriend go out dashing for you. Just get separate accounts.

Stealing Food

For in-person deliveries you must use the five-minute timer before leaving the food. You have to give the customer time to get to you. Yes, this can be frustrating sometimes, but it isn't worth losing your job over.

Also, and I hope it's self-evident, don't take food out of the bags, eat food, or simply not deliver it. You will lose your job very quickly.

Do Not Disclose Customer Information

Don't share names, pictures of houses or copies of text messages without blacking out the complete name and address.

Stickers

Do not open the bag for any reason. Certainly, don't open the bag to place your ratings sticker. Put it on the outside of the bag or simply use my text message tip to solicit ratings.

Misuse of the Red Card

No, you can't order a combo and keep the fries when the customer orders a burger and drink, even if it is cheaper.

Don't leave a tip when you use the Red Card to pay. I know it sucks, and I always feel stupid putting a 0 on the tip line, but the staff know it's DoorDash and they should know you can't tip.

Misusing the Referral Program

Don't solicit unsocial media, don't bulk send out etc. Give to direct friends only.

Turning Pro

Next Level

Now that you have the basics down and at least a few hours of dashing under your belt, it's time to look at turning pro. This next section is where the real money is made. Used together, these next suggestions can easily double your hourly earnings.

I would suggest trying these one at a time. Trying to implement all of them together can be overwhelming.

Dash Utility

If you have an Android phone there is a utility that makes life so much easier. Dash Utilities can help you auto decline small orders, auto accept large ones, and has a hand popup that shows the pay-out and dollars per mile for each offer. This app actually has dozens of features but those are the three that are most useful.

Voice Over

This is hit or miss. I don't always leave it on. But what it does is read out the order offer to you so you don't have to glance at the screen. What I wish it would do is allow me to use my voice to accept or deny the order.

Auto Accept

This allows you set basic parameters for orders you will always take - I set it pretty high because I don't like it to grab orders for me. Unfortunately, when it auto accepts it doesn't make a special noise to warn you you have an order.

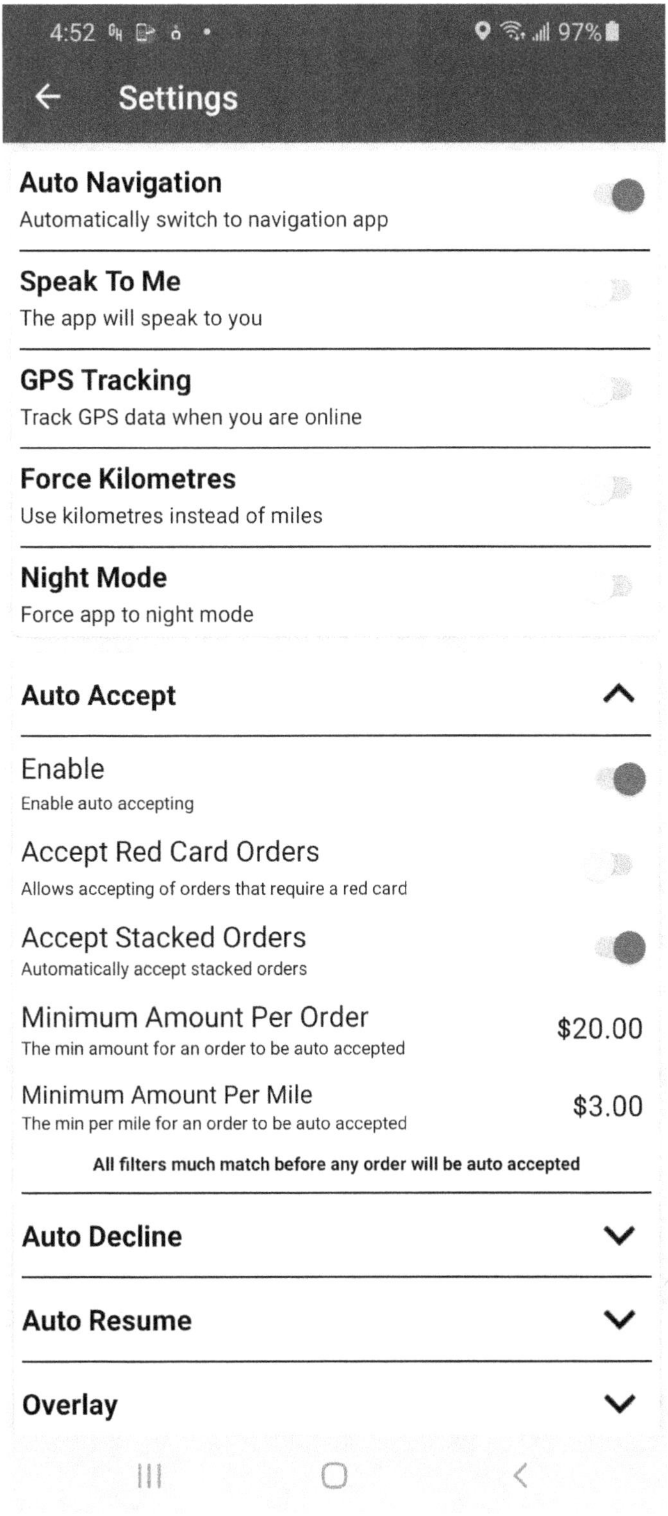

Auto Navigation
Automatically switch to navigation app

Speak To Me
The app will speak to you

GPS Tracking
Track GPS data when you are online

Force Kilometres
Use kilometres instead of miles

Night Mode
Force app to night mode

Auto Accept ⌃

Enable
Enable auto accepting

Accept Red Card Orders
Allows accepting of orders that require a red card

Accept Stacked Orders
Automatically accept stacked orders

Minimum Amount Per Order $20.00
The min amount for an order to be auto accepted

Minimum Amount Per Mile $3.00
The min per mile for an order to be auto accepted

All filters much match before any order will be auto accepted

Auto Decline ⌄

Auto Resume ⌄

Overlay ⌄

Auto Decline

This is why I use the app. You can set some parameters to auto decline orders. This saves you a ton of distraction. I highly recommend it.

← **Settings**

Auto Navigation
Automatically switch to navigation app

Speak To Me
The app will speak to you

GPS Tracking
Track GPS data when you are online

Force Kilometres
Use kilometres instead of miles

Night Mode
Force app to night mode

Auto Accept ⌄

Auto Decline ⌃

Decline Red Card Orders
When enabled it will decline ALL red card orders

Enable Auto Decline ⓘ
When enabled it will decline orders based on filters below

Minimum Amount Per Order $8.00
Any amount under this amount will be auto declined

Minimum Amount Per Mile $1.50
Any amount under this amount will be auto declined

ANY request that DOES NOT meet these filters will be auto declined

Auto Resume ⌄

Overlay ⌄

Pop Up

One of the nice things this app does is display a small popup over the Door Dash screen that display the destination address (very useful once you learn where the apartments are!) and a dollars per mile amount. Remember to aim for at least $1.50.

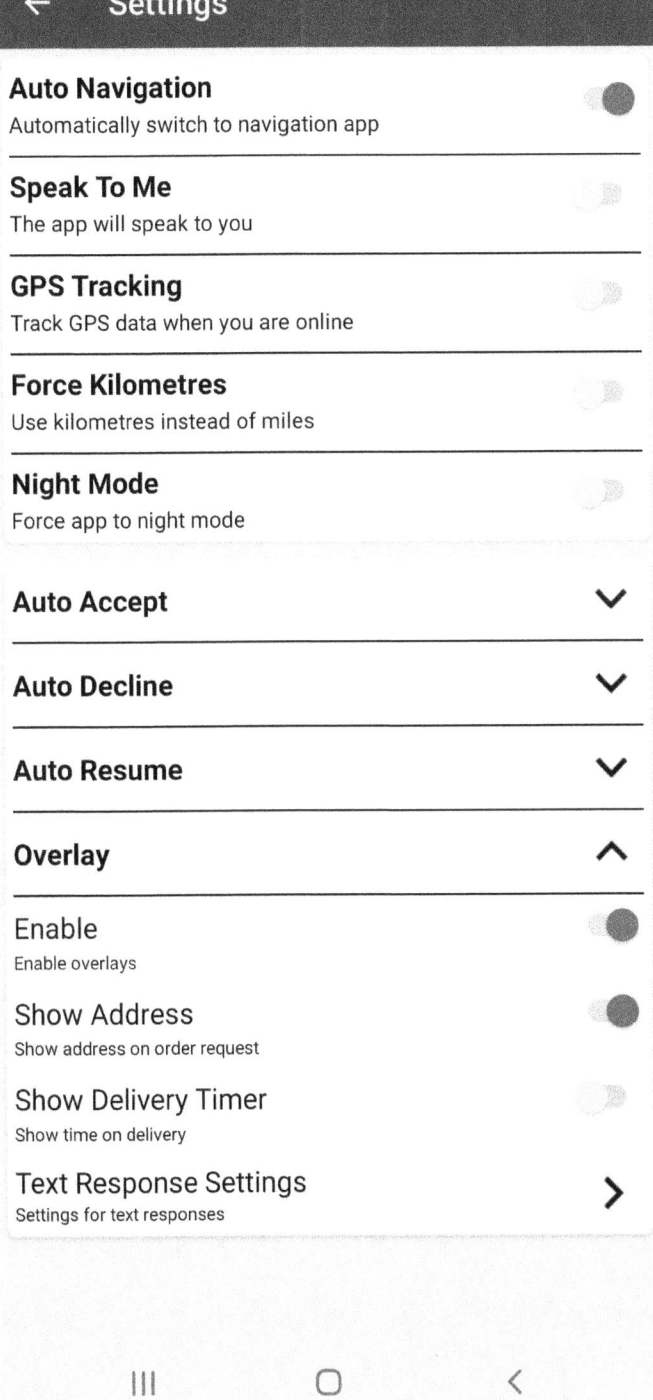

Settings

Auto Navigation
Automatically switch to navigation app

Speak To Me
The app will speak to you

GPS Tracking
Track GPS data when you are online

Force Kilometres
Use kilometres instead of miles

Night Mode
Force app to night mode

Auto Accept ⌄

Auto Decline ⌄

Auto Resume ⌄

Overlay ⌃

Enable
Enable overlays

Show Address
Show address on order request

Show Delivery Timer
Show time on delivery

Text Response Settings ❯
Settings for text responses

Where to download

You can grab this order from https://acceptordecline.com/

Multi App

The next trick in our arsenal is to multi app. In its simplest form multi-apping is simply running two or more different delivery services at once - i.e. DoorDash and Grubhub.

By running multi apps you decrease the amount of time you need to wait between orders, and you can - although I don't recommend it - accept orders on both apps at the same time. People do get deactivated for this. I would suggest not double dipping active deliveries.

What I do suggest doing is accepting an order on one system and after you pick the order up and are on the way to deliver, begin to watch new orders coming in on your other apps. Ideally, you will pick up a new order that is near where you are delivering. When this happens, you have no downtime and you can easily increase deliveries by 30-40%.

Be sure to pause the other app when you are on an order. Hearing dings for order offers from the other app can be distracting. Just unpause when you are on the way to the customer's house.

You really need to know your area for this to work well and be familiar with both apps.

Even if you think you don't want to multi app, I would still suggest signing up for a few other delivery services and occasionally delivering for them. Apps crash, you get deactivated or it's just a slow day. One or more of these will happen and you will be very glad you have a backup ready to go.

Tips

- Until you are very sure of your area and restaurants, only pick up a new order when you are on the way to drop off your current order.
- Know your area! Seriously, do not do this in an unfamiliar area.
- Keep an eye on delivery times - too many late deliveries can get you deactivated.
- Stacking orders on multi apps works but is stressful; one restaurant always seems to take forever. I do this for large amounts, but I don't like the added stress when orders are small.
- Every now and then you get lucky: one order on each app from the same restaurant to customers who are close to each other. I take those if the money is good.

Pro Tip

I'm just going to say it again - do not accept a second order on a different app until you are on the way to the customer's house with your current order.

Version Hack

Now that we've covered the basics let's look at how the pro's make money.

Wouldn't it make life easier if we didn't have to guess about the total pay-out for orders over $8.50? Of course it would - it makes dashing so much easier.

There is a way.

Before you get too excited, know that this only works for Android phones and it requires a few manual steps. It works so well that it is most likely worth it to grab a cheap Android phone for dashing if you are an iPhone user.

This hack requires you to install an older version of the Dasher app. After the old version is installed, when you receive an order you will see the total pay-out - including the full customer tip.

Here's how to do it:

Use your phone to download the old version from https://android-apk.org/com.doordash.driverapp/48859824-doordashdriver/

Uninstall the current version of Dasher.

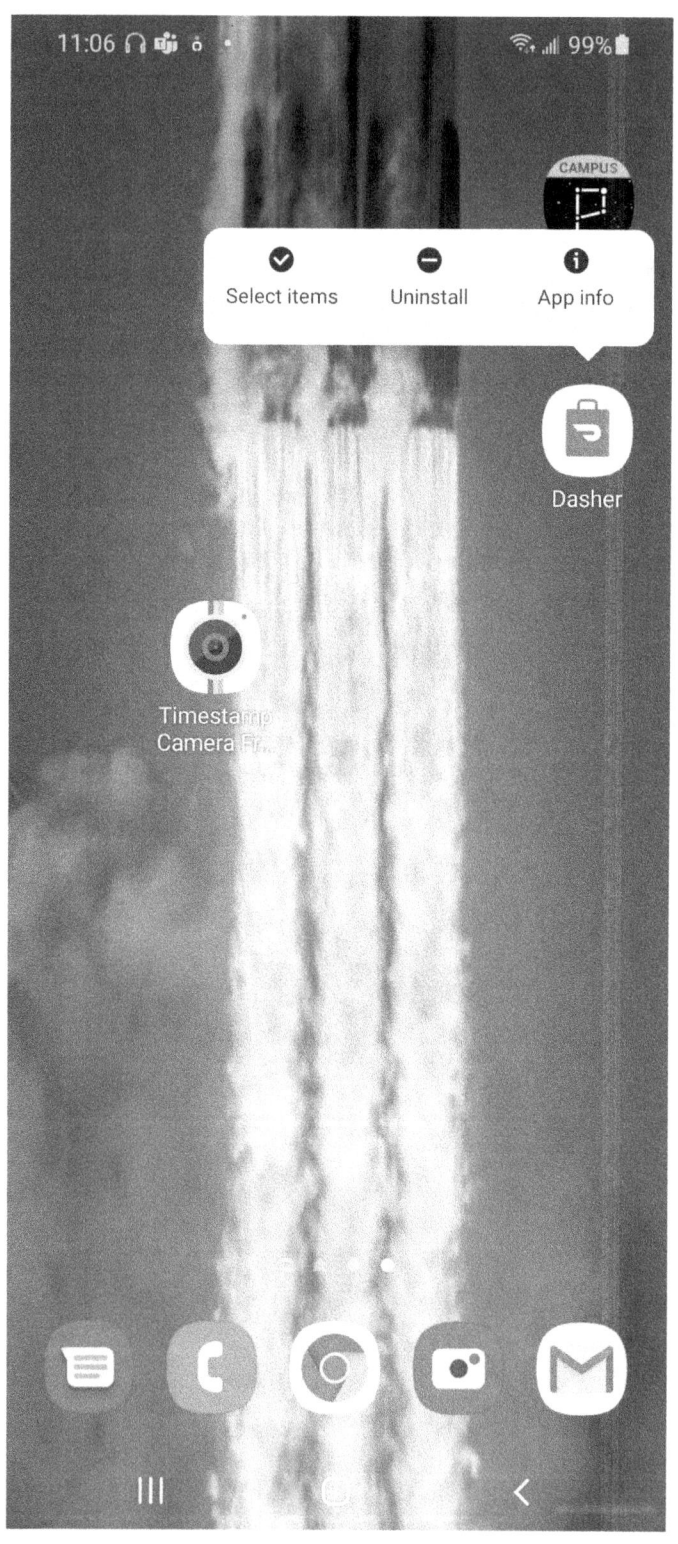

Turn off google play

Open Settings

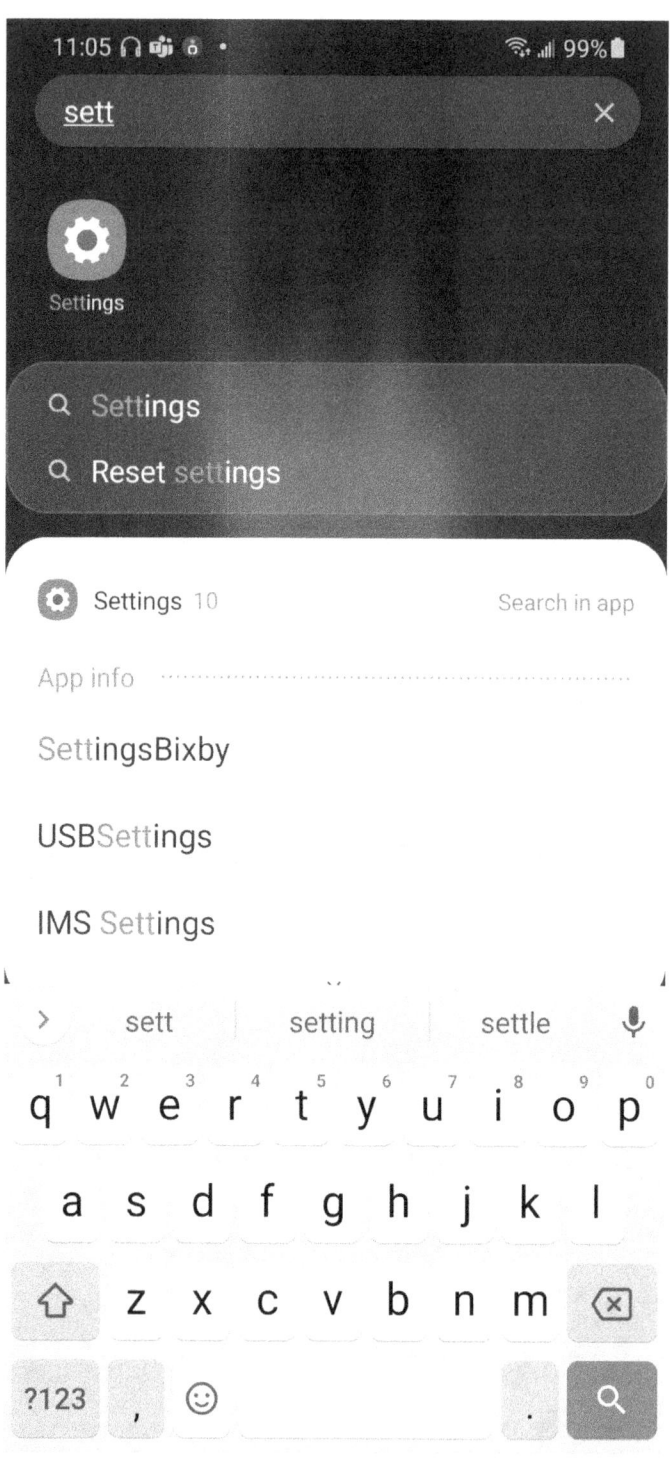

Search for 'Google Play"

< google play   ✕

Legal information
Google Play system update licenses

Biometrics and security
Google Play system update

Google Assistant
🎵   Music
Services used to play music

Security

App info
Google Play Games

App info
Google Play Store

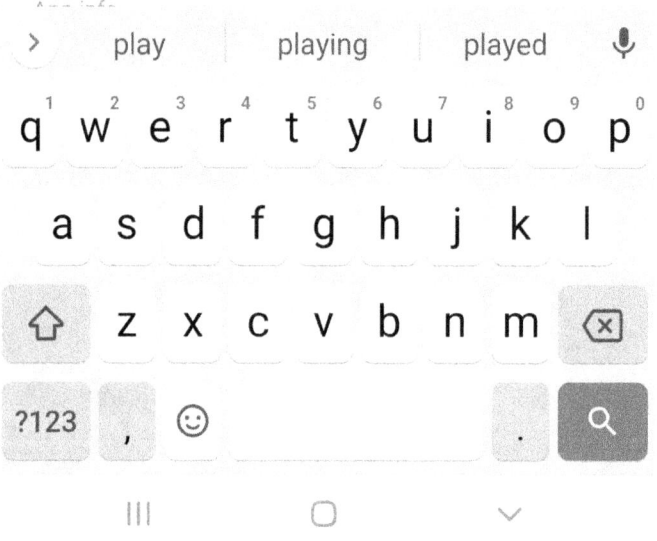

Select Disable

Google Play Store

Installed

Usage

Mobile data
805 MB used since Jun 1

Battery
0% used since last fully charged

Storage
117 MB used in Internal storage

Memory
133 MB used on average in last 3 hours

App settings

Notifications
Blocked

Permissions
Phone, SMS, and Storage

Open

Disable

Force stop

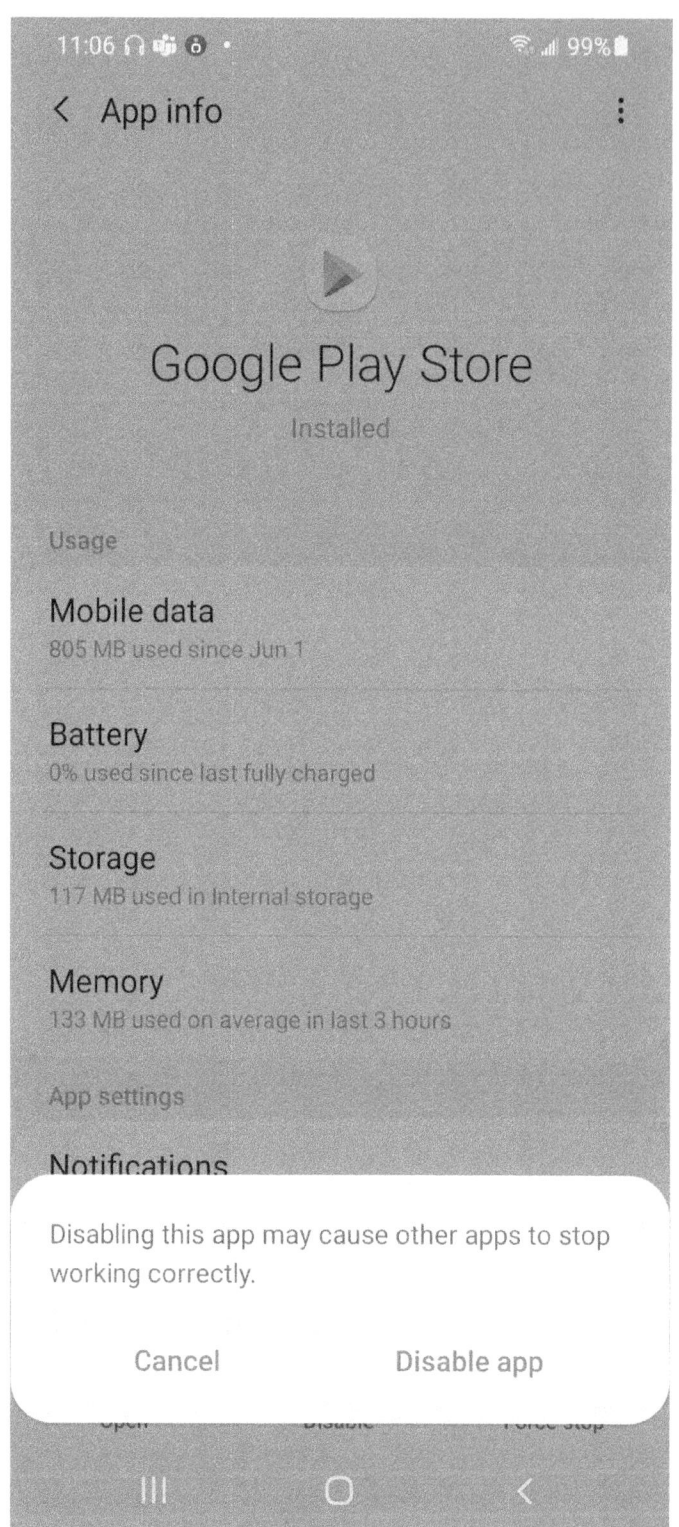

< App info ⋮

Google Play Store
Installed

Usage

Mobile data
805 MB used since Jun 1

Battery
0% used since last fully charged

Storage
117 MB used in Internal storage

Memory
133 MB used on average in last 3 hours

App settings

Notifications

Disabling this app may cause other apps to stop working correctly.

Cancel   Disable app

This is needed because the Dasher app attempts to update itself every time it runs. After we go through the steps, I'll tell you how I use Google Play and run the older version.

Now install the file you downloaded.

My Files

Q

Make the switch to OneDrive ✕

Switch from Samsung Cloud Drive to OneDrive to keep your important files safe and available on all your devices.

Get started

Recent files

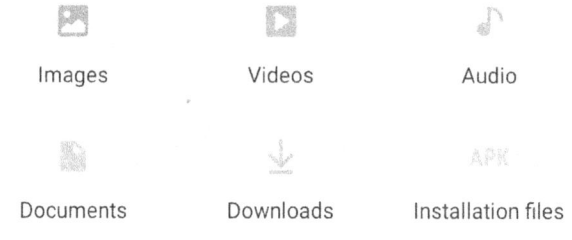

DD 5.63...-1.apk   mac-m...qs.pdf   jellysto...ns.pdf

Categories

Images	Videos	Audio

Documents	Downloads	Installation files

Internal storage
76.67 GB / 128 GB

SD card
Not inserted

||| ◯   ‹

You might receive a warning about downloading apps from unknown sources. If so, just click through it.

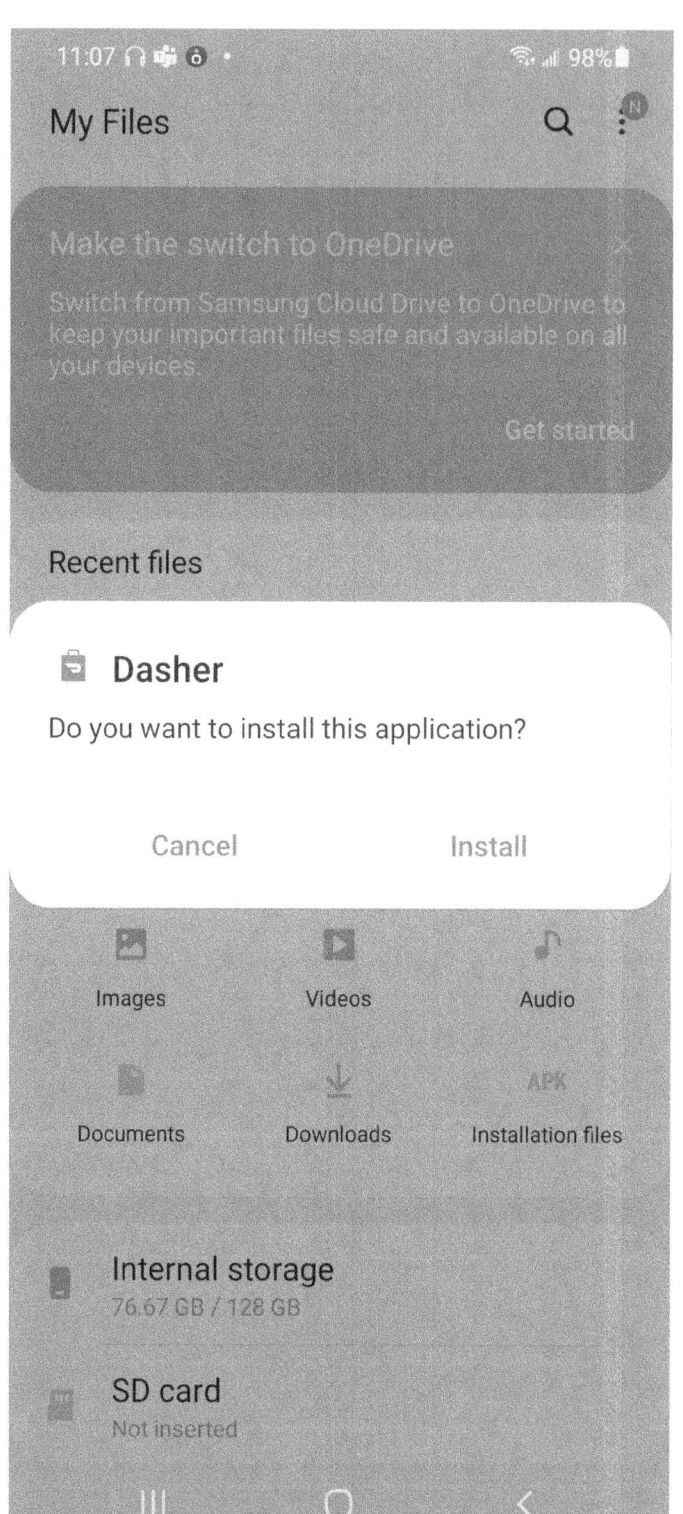

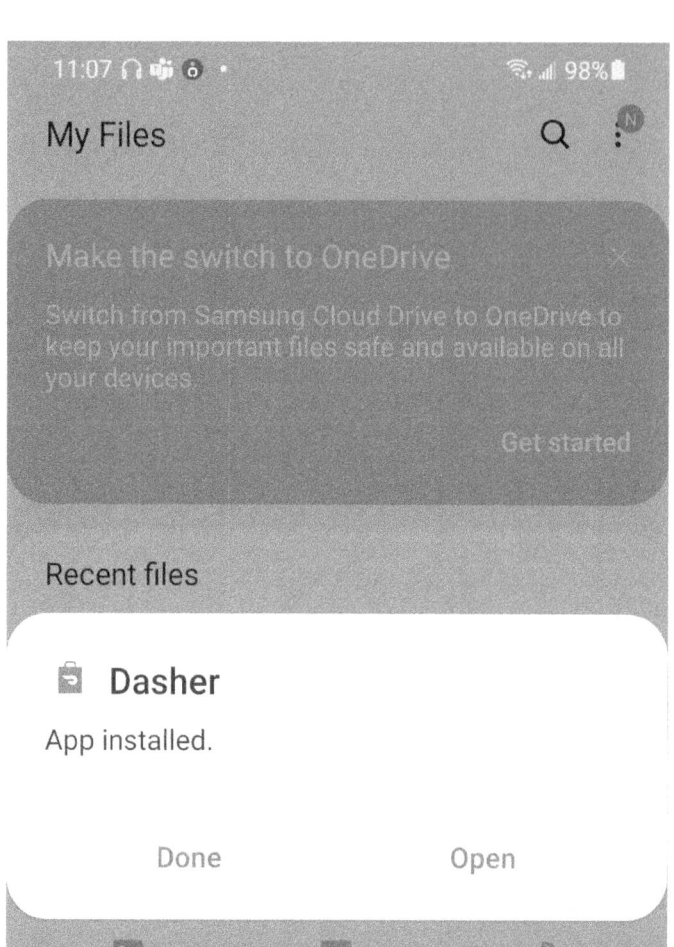

My Files

Recent files

Dasher

App installed.

Done   Open

Images   Videos   Audio

Documents   Downloads   Installation files

Internal storage
76.67 GB / 128 GB

SD card
Not inserted

70

Open the app and Log In

11:07 🎧 📱 🔒 ·　　🛜 .ıll 98% 🔋

Email

Password　　　　　　　　　🚫👁

Become a Dasher　　　　　Forgot Password?

SIGN IN

|||　　　○　　　＜

72

You want to see version 5.63.6

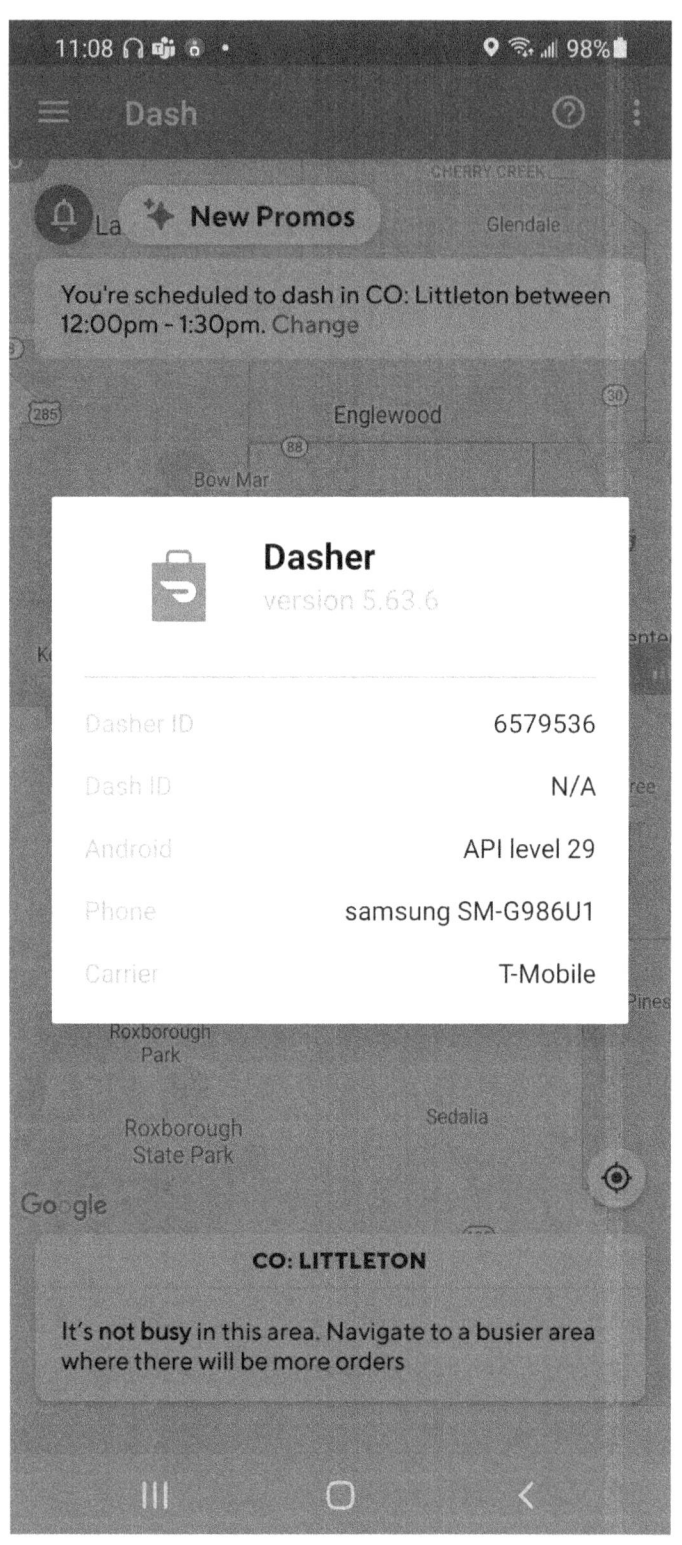

That's IT!

Run the old version of Dasher and you will see the total pay-out for each order.

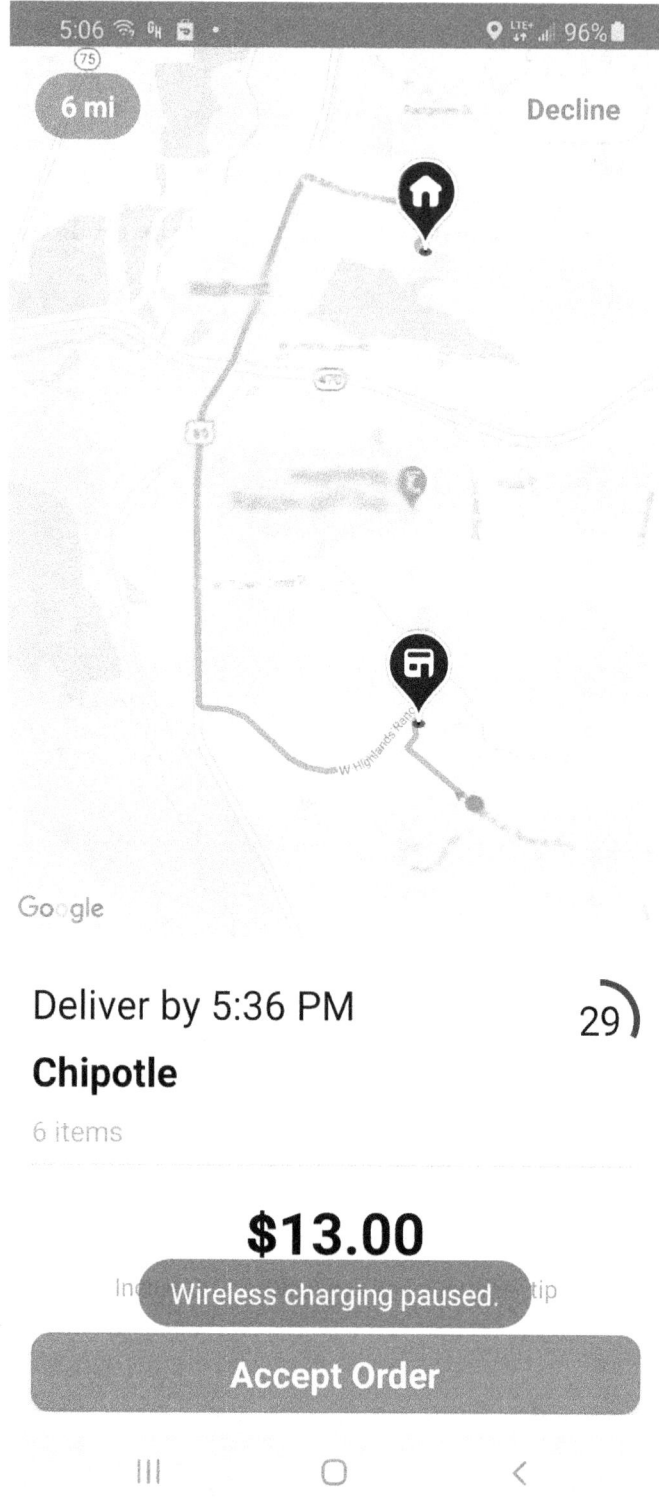

6 mi

Decline

Deliver by 5:36 PM

29

Chipotle

6 items

$13.00

Wireless charging paused.

Accept Order

I know these steps sound complex, but they really aren't. I'll reenable Google Play so that I can download more apps and update my existing one. Then when it's time to dash I simply disable it, delete the Dasher and reinstall the old version. It takes maybe a minute once you do it a few times.

Pro Tip

This won't last forever so don't build your life and earnings around this hack. Enjoy it while it's available but some day, a week or years from now, it will stop working.

#DECLINENOW

If you are on Facebook, you can join the #decinenow group. This is a group of dashers who are focused on getting DD to up their pay by declining all orders under seven dollars.

In fact, you will recognize a number of my basic recommendations if you spend any time on this group.

The group's core tenets are:

Repeat after me - AR does not matter and you do not have to accept every order - or any for that matter!

Pick you mileage and minimum and stick to it!

Never, ever, for any reason pick up a base order on the belief that the customer will tip in cash - it almost never happens.

Never accept an order less than $7.00 and adjust that number upwards if there is peak pay being offered.

Honestly, this group can be a little rough but it's good to occasionally drop in and see posts by like-minded people.

Pro Tip

Do not mention Top Dasher in this group... you've been warned.

Frequently Asked Questions

Is there any way to know if an order is going to an apartment?

Not specifically, the Order Offer screen does not give any indication. However, you'll soon learn that just by looking at the map you can largely know when it is an apartment delivery.

Should I wear DD shirts/hats?

No. Seriously, why?

How should I dress?

During the summer I wear shorts and t-shirts and in winter it's usually jeans and a sweatshirt. I see a few people who go business casual, but I've never understood why. I'm sure there has been a customer I've delivered to at least once who didn't like my dress, but no one has ever said a single thing. Be comfortable and clean and I think you are fine.

Do I have to have my bag?

No. You will see some restaurants list that you must have your bag, but I have never once been asked where it is. Other drivers like to carry it because they think the restaurant will get to them faster. That's really never been an issue with me so I don't worry about it.

Can I be deactivated for not accepting orders?

No. You are an independent contractor and can accept or decline any order offered to you. Once you accept an order you are contractually bound by the DoorDash terms of service to complete the order or utilize the approved method of unassigning an order. You can be deactivated for unassigning too many orders.

Can I be deactivated for being late?

Yes, but only in extreme cases. Keep your onetime delivery rate in the 90s and you should always be fine. It can occasionally happen that a restaurant is really late, you get lost, or traffic is horrendous. Stay in contact with your customer and in extreme cases contact DD support.

Can I be deactivated for unassigning orders?

You can be deactivated for a low completion rate so technically yes, but you won't be deactivated for unassigning an order on its own. Don't be afraid to unassign bad orders that you accidentally accepted. If I walk into a busy restaurant and they say we just got the order and it will be 10-15 minutes I almost always unassign unless it's a very high paying order. Give yourself some breathing room and try to keep your rate above 95%.

Should I sign up for multiple apps?

Yes, yes, and yes. First off, you really won't know which service is more popular in your area without trying them. Second, you need to do basic multi-tapping to increase your productivity and finally, you never know when you might be deactivated or the service could crash for the night. Keep multiple accounts going and you will always have a backup.

What is a DD Top Dasher and is it worth it?

A Top Dasher is someone who meets a lot of unreasonable requirements - most important of which is almost never declining an order. For that they get earlier access to scheduling blocks. You can't be a Top Dasher and a top earner at the same time. Taking 3-5 dollar orders all day to keep your acceptance rate up absolutely kills your earnings.

In some markets there are so many drivers that it might make sense to get access to early scheduling, but I would almost say it would be better to simply drive to another zone.

Some dashers will follow the earnings maximizing guidelines for most of the month and then in the last week or so take every order they are offered and attempt to get their acceptance rate up in time to make Top Dasher. This sounds exhausting to me but then I'm not doing this full-time.

Can I rate customers?

Nope!

Can I rate restaurants?

Nope!

Are hot spots worth it?

Maybe. Some people swear by them, others won't go near them. I recommend finding an area that is restaurant dense and either parking or driving around that area. I never specifically travel to a DD recommended hot spot.

Should I sit at a hot spot or drive around?

It depends on who you ask. I split the difference. I have a favorite parking spot that I will sit out in for 5-10 minutes. If I don't get an order I like then I will drive a small loop around the restaurants in that area and then park again.

Should I travel between areas for promotional bonuses?

It depends on where you live. If you are near a couple of zones, I would possibly pay attention to the bonus but in general I view them as a few extra bucks if they are active; I generally don't worry about them.

Should I accept orders that I have to pay for with my Red Card?

Usually it's no big deal. Keep in mind that every now and then the card can be declined, and it adds just a little more time to your pickup.

Should I accept orders that I have to place and then pay for?

Almost always no. When you know your area, you might occasionally get a large order with a good tip for a restaurant you know. I'll take those if it's a good pay-out.

Community

Reddit

You can find both DD driver subreddits as well as customer Reddits. The customer ones can sometimes be entertaining and will, every now and then, provide some insight that will allow you to do your job better.

The driver focused Reddits are mostly drivers complaining about no tips but from time to time there is a nugget of wisdom shared.

Facebook

As with Reddit, the Facebook groups are hit or miss and will be divided into both customer and driver focused groups.

State Level Facebook

By far, the most useful groups are ones that are more local. In Facebook and Reddit you can find local DD groups by simply searching for DoorDash and your state and sometimes city name.

YouTube

There are many energetic and sometimes even charismatic drivers posting videos. This is a great way to see deliveries in action and hear from some drivers who make a full-time living from DD. Most are bragging about how many hours they worked or the amount of money made but they almost always have some good tips. Personally, I would watch these videos before making too many deliveries:

Delivery Tips

Pro Dashing in a Nutshell

Decide on your metrics and stick to them.

Mark "arrived" when you reach the restaurant.

Be polite to restaurant staff.

Do not mark the order as picked up until you have the complete order in hand and you are in your car.

Double check for drinks!

Double check delivery instructions before leaving the restaurant - customers will often put special requests like "grab extra ketchup" in these comments.

Be nice to customers but you don't need to have a full-on conversation with them.

Take pictures of deliveries.

Set up text message macros - send a thank you for each order and if the order is contactless, a picture of the order on the porch. There are sample text message scripts at the end of this book.

If the customer responds, also wish them a good day and ask for a review.

Think about getting a body cam.

Change your car's oil and air filters on a regular schedule.

Make sure your tires are inflated properly.

Fill your car up at the end of each shift or at least put the gas in that you used.

Track your mileage - save yourself the hassle and just use a free app for this.

Look into buying gas from either Cosco or Sam's Club.

Use a cashback card when buying gas.

Download a gas app that shows you where the cheapest gas is.

Common Mistakes

Common Mistakes

Not tracking mileage.

Not keeping car maintenance up to date.

Not filling up after a dash.

Not declining quickly.

Not trying different dash times - generally lunch and dinner are the best but do you know what times? Is it 5:00-8:00pm or do the big orders start at 4:30pm. Experiment a little; you might be surprised.

Not documenting deliveries.

Not going directly to the restaurant.

Not multi-apping.

Not multi-apping in the correct way.

It is not a full-time job - pick your times.

Caring about your acceptance rate.

Taking long distance orders.

Taking low pay orders.

Traveling to a distant red zone just to start a shift.

Forgetting to pay quarterly taxes.

Not saving money to pay taxes.

Not having an emergency fund for car issues.

Not setting daily and weekly income goals.

Not scheduling blocks - schedule ahead of time to guarantee your ability to dash.

You need a fuel-efficient car.

Not documenting expenses for tax purposes.

Thinking DoorDash cares about you - there is always another driver.

No or low vehicle insurance - the delivery rider policy is low cost and you should have it.

Parking tickets.

Not being active on multiple delivery platforms.

Final Thoughts

There you have it. Everything I've learned. Now it's time to go and do it!

Drop me a line at prodasher@prodasher.com to let me know how it works for you and any new tips you have learned.

www.ingramcontent.com/pod-product-compliance
Lightning Source LLC
Chambersburg PA
CBHW071025220526
45467CB00004B/1516